Bassoon

Intermediate Level

MASTER SOLOS
by Leonard Sharrow

EDITED by Linda Rutherford

Contents

To access companion recorded performances
and accompaniments online, visit:
www.halleonard.com/mylibrary

Enter Code
5891-1495-2965-9569

ISBN 978-0-7935-9550-1

HAL•LEONARD®

Visit Hal Leonard Online at
www.halleonard.com

Contact Us:
Hal Leonard
7777 West Bluemound Road
Milwaukee, WI 53213
Email: info@halleonard.com

In Europe contact:
Hal Leonard Europe Limited
42 Wigmore Street
Marylebone, London, W1U 2RN
Email: info@halleonardeurope.com

In Australia contact:
Hal Leonard Australia Pty. Ltd.
4 Lentara Court
Cheltenham, Victoria, 3192 Australia
Email: info@halleonard.com.au

Two Sketches

musical terms

moderato	**moderately**
sostenuto	**sustained, smooth**
espressivo	**with expression**

The first selection in this book is a pair of contrasting solos that were composed especially for this series. The first study, "Reverie", is a fanciful, dreamlike piece. It should be performed in a smooth, flowing manner with sustained phrases and light tonguing where needed.

You will need to develop your ability more fully to play long tones and phrases which requires proper breathing and good breath support. It may help to think of the waist area as the bottom of a balloon. The throat and lips are similar to the neck and lip of the balloon. As air is allowed to escape from the balloon (lungs), the air is forced out by pressure all around. It is not only the diaphragm muscle that creates the pressure, but all of the muscles around your waist area: sides, back, and front.

Each time you practice begin by holding a long tone. By keeping a record of the time, you can increase the length and build your breath support.

In each of the solos in this book, you'll see markings like . . . . MM $\quad$=88. The M.M. stands for Maelzel's Metronome, the inventor of the metronome. This particular marking means that the metronome should be set at 88 and each click represents the length of a quarter note.

These indications are suggestions of a tempo. If at first you cannot play the solo at this tempo, practice it slower and gradually increase the speed as you learn it. If this tempo is too fast for you and your accompanist to perform well, play it at a speed that is comfortable for both of you.

When you are listening to the solos on your cassette, you'll notice that many of the longer tones seem to "fluctuate" or "pulsate" (have a rolling effect.) This is called vibrato, a technique used by vocalists, string and wind instrumentalists to make the tone quality warmer and more expressive. It is an essential technique for a good bassoonist, but should be used only after a full, rich tone quality has already been established.

By playing a series of "forte-pianos", playing loud and getting immediately soft, in a controlled sequence, you begin to get the feel of the vibrato. Try the following exercise at about $\quad$. = 66. Put an accent, using the breath, on the downbeat of each measure and immediately get soft. Make sure the sound does not stop. Think that the tone looks like this ⌣⌣⌣ rather than this ⋀⋀⋀ .

PREPARATION 1

After you can control the "forte-pianos" at the slower speed, practice putting two pulsations on each beat. Each time you can regulate the vibrato, add another pulsation to each beat so that you play three, four, etc.

PREPARATION 2

After you have learned to start an exercise with vibrato, begin without vibrato and gradually add it. As you come to the end of the exercise, slow the pulsations until there is no vibrato.

PREPARATION 3

No Vibrato   Vibrato   No Vibrato

All of these exercises should be practiced in all registers of the instrument and at various dynamic levels.

A number of factors will affect how you use vibrato: the register in which you are playing, the length of the note, the intensity of the note within the phrase, and with what instruments you are playing. Generally, a higher note will demand a faster vibrato than a lower note, and a shorter note will also need a faster vibrato. It is quite possible that the most intense note within a phrase will be in the low register, but will need a faster vibrato because of its intensity.

Finally, the instrumentation and situation will dictate the use of vibrato. If you are playing in an ensemble and your part is a harmony part, do not use vibrato. Also listen to the instruments with which you are playing. If they do not use vibrato, such as clarinet, you should use very little so the tone qualities blend. As you learn to control your vibrato and listen to other players, you will learn instinctively how and when to use this technique.

Measures 1-20   In several measures of this solo there will be a change of meter. The easiest way to count these changes is to think of the quarter note beat. This will remain constant. For each measure count two or three quarter notes to the measure depending on the time signature. In measures 1-3 the time signature is 3/4 and in measure 4 it changes to 2/4. Remember that the metronome markings are suggestions of a tempo. You should play at a tempo that is comfortable for you and your accompanist. During your measures of rest count very carefully so you will enter correctly. Prepare for your entrances early — set your embouchure, get your fingers in position, and take your breath. When you do this, the notes will not seem to begin so suddenly or explode. The phrase "sostenuto espressivo" at the beginning indicates that this solo is to be played sustained and expressively.

You should strive to play eight measures with one breath to connect the phrases. Until you build up your breath support, you could take a breath every four measures. Watch the dynamic and articulation markings very carefully throughout the solo. Practice the following exercise which uses different time signatures. Try to play as many measures as possible with one breath.

PREPARATION 4

Measures 21-36 A slightly different musical idea is introduced by the piano in measure 21. This theme may seem faster because the notes are of smaller values. Be sure that you or your accompanist do not speed-up. The sustained, expressive quality remains in this section.

Measures 37-57 The first theme returns in these measures. Remember the points discussed earlier when playing this part. The end is similar to the introduction with the accompaniment dying away to nothing.

musical terms

// (caesura)	**pause**
allegro	**quickly**
con spirito	**with spirit**
marcato	**in a marked and emphatic style**
simile	**in the same manner until there is a change indicated**

In contrast to the "Reverie", the "Peasant Dance" is moderately fast, spirited, and strongly articulated. "Marcato" means in a stressed, emphatic manner. As in the "Reverie", there are several changes in meter. Although the time signature is 4/4, the tempo is ♩ = 104. The composer wants the piece to have the feeling of two strong beats in the 4/4 measures. It is also impractical to set the metronome for four beats because of the speed. When you get to a 3/4 measure, play the quarter notes at the same tempo but, instead of playing four quarter notes in a measure, play only three. Similarly, a 2/4 measure equals two quarter notes.

Measures 1-16 Begin "forte" and emphasize each note. In measure 3 you'll see the word "simile" which tells you to continue playing marcato — stressed and emphatic. Your accompanist should also play in the same manner, accented and stressed.

Measures 17-24 This section should be a little softer and quieter but still with the driving spirit. In measure 19 double grace notes are used. You already know that grace notes are small decorative notes played ahead of the beat. These double grace notes are played like the others, quickly just before the principle note. Practice the following grace note exercise.

PREPARATION 5

At the end of measure 24 you'll see two diagonal lines, // These are called "caesura" in Italian or "railroad tracks" in English and tell you to pause briefly before going on to measure 25.

Measures 25-41 The opening theme is repeated, beginning in this measure. Remember to play it spirited and strongly articulated. Be sure that you do not slow down at the end.

Two Sketches

Reverie

Edmund J. Siennicki

Peasant Dance

Chanson Triste

musical terms

a tempo   **in tempo, in time, return to the tempo which precedes a rit.**
legato   **smoothly connected**

new notes

G

High

A♭

High

One of the most outstanding composers of the Romantic period of music history (1825-1900) was the Russian, Peter Tchaikovsky. He lived and composed at the same time as several other Russian composers whose writings were considered nationalistic, based on the music indigenous to the country. Tchaikovsky's compositions were comparatively free of this influence. He used his background more as a flavor or exotic accent. His compositions are extremely lyrical and full of expression.

This beautiful solo was originally written for piano and arranged for the bassoon. It should be played with a broad flowing line and a singing tone quality. All repeated notes should be tongued softly, but distinctly. Use legato tonguing, think of saying the syllable "da" instead of "ta", throughout the solo.

Measures 1-12   Listen to the accompaniment in the first four measures. This will indicate the tempo and the dynamic level you should match when you enter. Also, use the introduction to prepare for your first note so it will not "explode" or be too loud to suit the solo. Watch all of the dynamic markings very closely and play wide ranges of expression throughout.

Measures 13-24   In this section you'll be using a new clef sign — the tenor clef ( ). Because the bassoon has such a wide range, this clef is often used to avoid too many ledger lines. When you first began playing the bassoon, you learned that with a bass clef sign at the beginning of a line, a note on a certain line or space is always the same note. This is also true of the tenor clef. Study the illustration which shows the relationship of the tenor clef to the bass and treble clefs. The two curved lines on the tenor clef outline "C" which is shown by the first ledger line below the treble clef and the first ledger line above the bass clef.

ILLUSTRATION 1

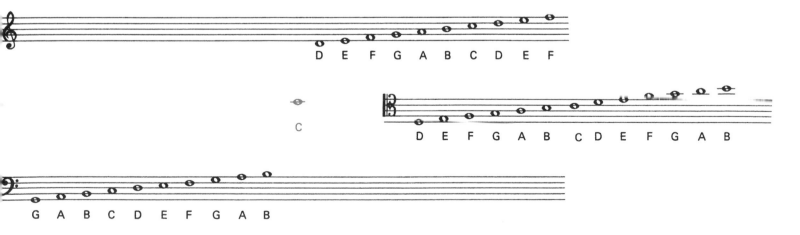

After you learn the names of the lines and spaces, you'll find playing in this clef just as easy as playing in the bass clef. Since the melody is very scale-like in this particular song, listening to the melody will also be a help in learning the tenor clef. Practice the exercises below to become familiar with the names of the lines and spaces in tenor clef. In each the corresponding bass clef notes will be shown on a small staff.

PREPARATION 7

Watch very carefully when moving from bass clef to tenor clef and back. Each time there is a change in the clef sign, the new clef sign will be shown immediately before the change.

Measures 25-34 Beginning in this measure a new melodic idea is introduced. Use the four-measure rest to take a breath, relax your embouchure briefly, and prepare for your entrance at measure 29. Play this section slightly louder than the first. Crescendo to the first note of measure 33. Then put a slight space (take a quick breath if you need it) between the first and second notes of the measure. Measures 33, 34, and 35 are the high point of the solo and should be played "forte". In measure 37 the movement from the "F" to "Bb", back to "Eb", must be as smooth as possible. Remember to "flick" your left thumb on the "Bb" to help the note speak clearly. This "Bb" could also be slightly sharp in pitch so you may need to "lip it down" (relax your lower jaw slightly to adjust the pitch). Decrescendo on the next three measures to finish off this section.

Measures 40-52 Again use your five measures of rest to relax your embouchure and fingers and to prepare for your next entrance. When you enter at measure 45, the accompaniment has the melody and the solo part is a countermelody that fits with it. This countermelody is a contrast to the melody and should be softer. Watch the articulation markings in this part. Every two measures is slurred, so work at making the phrases smooth and connected.

Measures 53-64 The original melody returns to the solo part in measure 53. You'll be moving into the tenor clef again in this part. Remember to think about the movement of the melodic line in these measures.

Measures 65-72 The notes in measures 65, 67, and 71 have tenuto marks. They should be stressed slightly and held for their full value with a very small space between them. Measures 67 and 68 are an exact repeat of measures 65 and 66. Make the second two measures softer for contrast. Put a crescendo and decrescendo on the last two measures even though they are very soft. Indicate the release of the last note to your accompanist with a small up-down motion of your instrument.

Chanson Triste

Peter Tchaikovsky
(1840-1893)

Arioso and Humoreske

musical terms

langsam	**slowly**
dolce	**sweetly**
stringendo	**accelerating, usually suddenly**
morendo	**Italian for dying; diminuendo or decrescendo**

Julius Weissenborn, one of the most prominent composers for the bassoon, lived in Germany during the late 1800's. His bassoon method was published in 1887. In addition to composing, Weissenborn was the first bassoonist of the Leipzig Gewandhaus Orchestra and a professor at the Conservatory in Leipzig.

Although he lived during the Romantic period of music history, the 19th century, he was extremely influenced by the Classical period which preceded the Romantic period.

In "Arioso and Humoreske", characteristics from both periods are represented. The "Arioso" is written in the style of the Romantic period. It is a smooth, quiet piece with some motion in the two "stringendo" passages. In contrast, the "Humoreske" portrays the light, clean characteristics of the Classical period. It has a definite rhythmic pulse and a wide contrast of dynamics.

The "Arioso" should be played smoothly connected with much breath support. The term "langsam" tells you it should be played slowly and "dolce", sweetly. Any separations should be played with a legato tongue. Think of using the syllable "da" instead of "ta".

Measures 1-8   Prepare for each of your entrances early so the sound does not "explode", especially since it is marked "piano". In measure 3 the legato markings (staccato under a slur) tell you to separate these notes using legato tonguing. Crescendo and decrescendo the half note and play the last eighth note of the measure long, so it leads into the next measure.

Measures 9-16   Crescendo the long "B" in this measure. By playing a crescendo and using more of a breath accent on the "B" on the second beat, measure 10 will not seem to explode. It should sound like the culmination of the crescendo already started in measure 9.

Measures 17-24 Measure 17 begins a one-measure "stringendo" section. The tempo should be increased slightly but, because it is only one measure, don't make the acceleration too noticeable. With the "a tempo" in measure 18, the tempo that preceded the "stringendo" returns. A new rhythm is introduced in measure 20. The "E" has two dots after it so it equals 1 3/4 of a beat. Practice the following exercise using the double-dotted quarter note. In the first measure it has been notated as a quarter note tied to one eighth and one sixteenth. In other measures it is shown as it is usually written.

PREPARATION 8

Measures 25-29 Again a one-measure "stringendo" occurs in measure 25. Be sure there is a slight speeding-up in this measure, returning to the "a tempo" in measure 26. The "B" to "A" in measure 27 must be slurred. To help the "A" speak, flip the thumb key lightly. The last note marked with "morendo" should diminuendo until it fades away.

musical terms

tempo 1	**return to the original tempo of a solo**
commodo	**leisurely, at an easy pace**
animato	**with spirit, animated**
accel.	**accelerando, growing faster**

new notes

The second part of the solo, the "Humoreske", is a light, clean composition. The tempo should not be too fast, "commodo" means convenient or comfortable.

Measures 1-8   The rhythmic pattern using two slurred notes is characteristic of this movement. The dot on the last note of each group tells you that the note should be short. It may help if you stress the first note. Because the last note is short, there will be a slight space after each group. Keep the rhythm very steady so each group begins exactly on the beat. Practice the following exercise using this articulation.

PREPARATION 9

There are several places where there are large skips slurring up to "A", such as measures 2, 10, 18, 19, 20, 21, 22, 23, 26, 34, 42, 50, and 53. Whenever you are slurring to the "A", be sure to "flip" or "flick" this note to get a good, smooth slur.

Measures 9-16   Build this second phrase to the "forte" in measure 13 and be careful not to change the tempo in any way.

Measures 17-24 Measure 17 begins the "animato", a livelier, spirited section. Begin softly but play the articulations and accents very carefully. Remember to "flick" the slurred "A's" as before. At the end of measure 24, you'll notice the two parallel lines, "railroad tracks". Remember to pause briefly before going on to measure 25.

Measures 25-44 The original tempo, Tempo I, returns at measure 25. Watch the dynamic and articulation markings in this section. The two-note slur pattern is again prominent and should be played as it was earlier.

Measures 45-52 Beginning in measure 45 the last beat of each measure is a quarter note which creates a secondary melodic line. Project each of these notes, but connect each measure to the next. Put a slight crescendo on these measures to the last quarter note of measure 52.

Measures 53-56 Use your one measure rest to prepare for the last phrase. Set your embouchure and fingers, think of the pitch of the note "A", and take your breath. Since this phrase should start softly, this preparation will help

prevent the note from being too loud. In measure 55 there is a new rhythm, the dotted eighth-sixteenth note. The dotted eighth is equal to three tied sixteenth notes and it customary to put a slight space after the dotted eighth note. Think of the third sixteenth note of a beat as a rest, instead of a note. A sixteenth rest looks like this γ and is equal to 1/4 of a beat. In the exercise below, the first measure shows the rhythm of this figure as it should sound. The rest of the exercise is notated as a dotted eighth and sixteenth note If a song is slower and more lyrical, the dotted eighth note would not be played quite as short.

PREPARATION 10

In measures 55 and 56 the "animato" indicates that you should speed-up slightly to finish the solo.

Arioso and Humoreske

Julius Weissenborn
(1837 - 1888)

Humoreske

Three Baroque Dances

Joseph Bodin de Boismartier was a French composer during the Baroque period of music history. He was born in France in 1691 and during his lifetime composed several operas, a number of cantatas, and a large number of instrumental works. These three dances were probably a part of the music from one of his operas.

The gavotte is a dance, originally from France. It is in a moderate 4/4 or 2/2 tempo and the phrases usually begin and end with an upbeat or pick-up.

Measures 1-4   Give your accompanist a cue so you will start together on the dance. This should be played vigorously with strong, but not short, articulation on any notes that are not slurred. Each time a phrase begins, try to accent the beat that comes at the beginning of the measure. This will bring out the upbeat of each phrase. You should play all repeats when you are playing with your accompanist. All second endings were taken in this solo

so the entire solo could be recorded on the tape. Watch the dynamics and make a contrast in the repeat.

Measures 5-7   Begin this section "forte". Remember the articulation must be strong. When you are playing the skips from lower notes to higher notes as in measure 5, you will need to listen carefully and support the "C" so it will be in tune. Be sure to slur all four eighth notes in measure 6.

Measures 8-12   The last part of measure 8 is the beginning of the third phrase and it is built around the pattern of two slurred eighth notes. Again on any intervals moving to the high "B", "C", or "D", you may need to "flip" the thumb key to help the notes speak. On the first beat of measure 12 you'll see a "+" above the "B". This is one symbol for a mordent. A mordent is an embellishment of two to four notes played before the written note. It uses the principle (written) note and the nearest upper scale note with an accent on the first note of the group. In this particular song the mordent should contain two notes. Look at the illustration below which shows the mordent as it is notated in measures 12 and 13; then as it would be written out.

ILLUSTRATION 2

WRITTEN  = PLAYED

Measures 12-16 Be sure you start this phrase with the correct articulation. Only three of the eighth notes are slurred, the last eighth should be tongued. On the repeat of this section ritard. slightly.

The second and third dances are both minuets. The minuet is an old dance form which is stately, not too fast, and always has a time signature with three beats to a measure — 3/4 or 3/8. Remember that the bottom number in the time signature tells you what kind of note gets one beat, so in 3/8 the eighth note gets one beat. Very often in the Baroque period when a pair of minuets appeared, the first minuet was played after the second to complete the solo. This is indicated in the solo by D.S. al Fine.

Measures 1-9   The first minuet begins with a full, rich sound and clear articulation. Watch the pattern of two slurred notes and be sure to tongue the first note of each.

Measures 10-17 Begin the second phrase softly. Since there are no slurs in the first part of this section, keep the articulation clear and definite, but not too harsh.

Measures 18-26 Start to crescendo in this measure building to the "C" in the last measure. In measure 21 there is another mordent that would look like this if written out.

ILLUSTRATION 3

Remember to play this mordent right before the beat. Make a difference between the three slurred notes and the three tongued notes that occur in measures 22, 23, and 24. The first "C" in the last measure should be "forte" and the second "C" a little softer so the phrase will sound finished.

Measures 1-9 There should be very little break between the first and second minuets and both should be played at the same tempo. The second minuet is written in the key of C minor. This means that the song is built around a minor scale. You've already studied major scales and key signatures. Look at the illustration below.

ILLUSTRATION 4

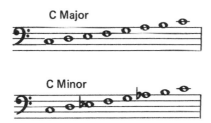

You'll notice that compared to the major scale, this minor scale has a lowered third step and a lowered sixth step. This is the reason a composition in a minor key sounds different than a composition in a major key. In this particular solo, the first minuet is written in C major so the second minuet will sound different. Remember both minuets are the same tempo, so don't let the second one slow down because of the change of key, the "piano" dynamic marking, and the legato style.

In measure 3 connect the "C" to "C" skip with legato tonguing and "flipping" the thumb key if necessary. Watch all articulation markings carefully.

Measures 10-16 This section should be slightly louder than the first phrase. In measure 13 there is a mordent. The flat sign above the plus tells you that the upper note should be an "A♭" in this case.

ILLUSTRATION 5

Measures 17-26 Begin to crescendo in this measure, building to the "forte" in measure 23. Keep the dynamic level at "forte" until the last note, which has a small decrescendo. Put a slight ritard. on the last two measures.

Pause slightly before you go back to the first minuet to finish the solo.

Review the points discussed earlier for the first minuet. Also ritard. on the last few measures of this minuet to close.

Three Baroque Dances

Gavotte

Joseph de Boismortier
(1691-1765)

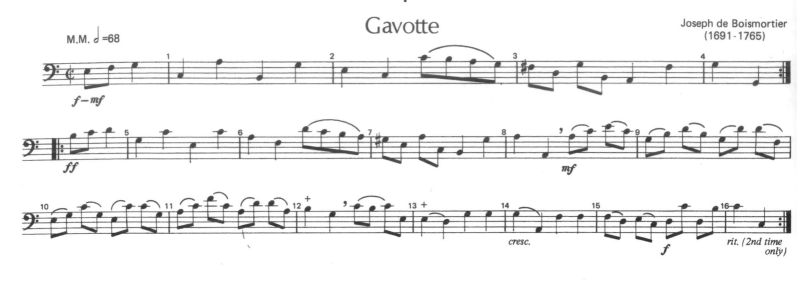

Menuet I

Menuet II

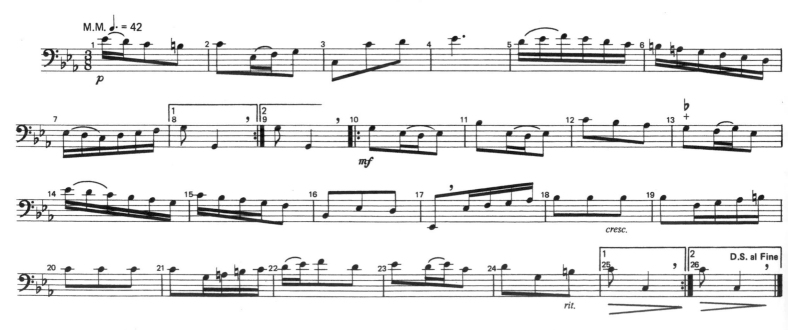

Sonata No. 5

musical term

adagio   **slowly, leisurely**

new notes

C#   D

trill (C fingering)   trill (D fingering)

Johann Galliard was an oboist and composer, who lived in the latter part of the Baroque period. For some time he was the chapel-master for the royal family in England. He became overshadowed by the other composers of the Baroque period and retired to a less active life. He was asked later to composer the music for several operas and cantatas.

This sonata follows the structure of the later "sonata de chlesa" (sonata of the church), slow-fast-slow-fast. Originally the "sonata de chiesa" had no dance forms in it, but later these forms were added.

On the tape, second endings were played throughout. When you are performing, you should observe both the first and second endings.

Measures 1-7   The first movement is "adagio", slow, with a metronome marking of ♪=80. Even though the time signature is 4/4, it will be easier to subdivide and count eight beats to a measure. Play the entire movement

smooth and connected with a legato tongue. In the first measure there is a dotted quarter note followed by two sixteenths. This is the same rhythm you have already learned with the eighth note divided into two equal parts. In this movement don't rush the sixteenths. Whenever a pick-up to a new phrase or motive occurs, try to think of it as carrying you forward. These occur in several measures. Notice how many notes are to be slurred. Whenever a note is at the end of a phrase or motive and followed by an eighth rest, decrescendo slightly and don't stop it abruptly with your tongue or breath. In measure 7 you have a new rhythm using thirty-second notes. Eight thirty-second

notes equal one quarter note beat. ♩=▤▤ ▤▤ In this figure two thirty-seconds come right after the beat.

On the second beat of this measure there is a trill. A trill is the rapid alternation of the principle (written) note and the next scale note above it. In Baroque music, it is general practice to start the trill on the upper neighbor, alternate with the principle note, and stop on the principle note before continuing. The trill also starts slowly and then increases in speed. The illustration below shows you measure 7 in the written notation and the notes that should be played.

ILLUSTRATION 6

WRITTEN   PLAYED

   =   

To prepare for this trill, practice the following exercise. Set the metronome at ♩=60 at first, later practice at a faster speed. The beat is divided into two, three, four, six, and eight equal parts. Strive to make the exercise as even as possible.

PREPARATION 11

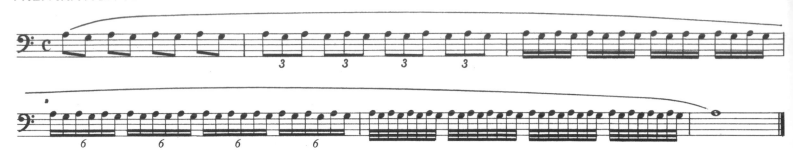

Measures 8-16   The second phrase of the movement begins in this measure with a melodic structure very similar to the beginning. In measure 10 there are three "B's" which must be separated. Use a legato tongue on all of these and slightly stress the one "B♭" which has an accent. In measure 11 there is another accented note which also should be stressed. On both of these, try using the breath to accent the note, rather than hitting the reed with the tongue. The trill in measure 13 would look like the illustration below if written out.

ILLUSTRATION 7

For the trill in measure 13, use the trill fingering shown above. Finger the "C♯" with the fingering shown, and lift the third finger of the left hand to trill "D".

musical term

e spiritoso   **with spirit**

Measures 1-7   There should be only a slight pause between the first and second movements. Since the solo and the accompaniment begin together, you will have to give a cue to begin the second movement. To get the tempo set, you may want to cue the first three notes. The staccatos in this movement should be separated, but not extremely short. Think of putting a small space between the notes. Remember that the word "simile" tells you the same articulation should be observed until there is a change indicated.

Measures 8-12   This section should start softly. On the eighth and two sixteenth note figure, think of each progressing into the quarter note which follows. These quarter notes form a descending scale. Beginning with the pick-up in measure 9, crescendo each group of sixteenth notes to the "forte" on the low "D". Practice these sixteenth notes slowly at first to make them as smooth and even as possible. When you are performing this solo, don't forget to repeat this section.

MASTER SOLOS
INTERMEDIATE
LEVEL
**Edited & Performed
by Leonard Sharrow**

Bassoon

HAL•LEONARD®

MASTER SOLOS

by Leonard Sharrow

EDITED by Linda Rutherford

Contents

ISBN 978-0-7935-9550-1

Visit Hal Leonard Online at
www.halleonard.com

Contact Us:
Hal Leonard
7777 West Bluemound Road
Milwaukee, WI 53213
Email: info@halleonard.com

In Europe contact:
Hal Leonard Europe Limited
42 Wigmore Street
Marylebone, London, W1U 2RN
Email: info@halleonardeurope.com

In Australia contact:
Hal Leonard Australia Pty. Ltd.
4 Lentara Court
Cheltenham, Victoria, 3192 Australia
Email: info@halleonard.com.au

Two Sketches

Edmund J. Siennicki

Reverie

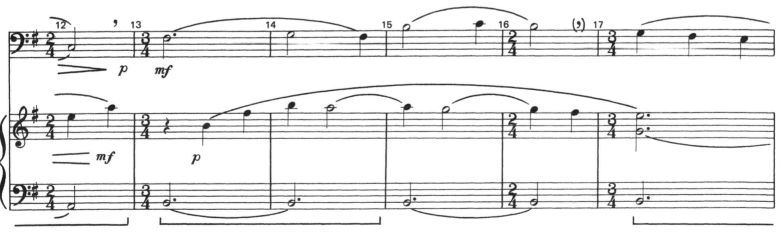

Peasant Dance

6

Chanson Triste

Peter Tchaikovsky
(1840-1893)

Arioso and Humoreske

Arioso

Julius Weissenborn
(1837-1888)

11

Humoreske

15

Three Baroque Dances

Joseph de Boismortier
(1691-1765)

Gavotte

Menuet I

Menuet II

(M.M. 𝅘𝅥𝅭 = 42)

19

Sonata No. 5

Johann Ernst Galliard
(1680-1749)

Romanze

Edmund J. Siennicki

($\quarternote$ = 80)
Allegretto

Menuetto
Piano Sonata no. 11, op. 22

Ludwig von Beethoven
(1770-1827)

Two Impromptus

Edmund J. Siennicki

38

Measures 13-21 The staccatos in this section should be the same as they were in the first, separated, but not too short. Watch all articulation and dynamic markings carefully.

Measures 22-30 The figure in measure 22 should begin "mezzo forte" followed by the same figure an octave lower in measure 23. This repetition should be very soft. Beginning in measure 24 the eighth and two sixteenths occur again. As before, think of each of these figures as moving toward the quarter note which follows. Beginning with the pick-up in measure 27 crescendo to the high "F" in measure 29. The repeat of this second section is optional, but on the last time through, the section ritards slightly.

musical terms

alla	**in the style of**
Siciliano	**dance of Sicilian peasants**

Measures 1-9 The third movement of this sonata is a siciliano, a dance originally from Sicily. It is moderately slow and has a 6/8 or 12/8 time signature.

This movement should be lyrical and flowing. The dotted eighth-sixteenth-eighth note rhythm is new. Divide the first three beats of the measure into six sixteenth notes. The dotted eighth would be equal to three sixteenths tied together, followed by a sixteenth note. The last eighth note comes on the last two sixteenths or beat 3. Practice the following exercise using different rhythms in 6/8 time.

PREPARATION 12

19

Whenever you have this figure in the solo, strive to make the last eighth note lead into the next beat. It should not be short. In measure 2 the quarter note comes on beats 1 and 2 and the two sixteenths on beat 3. Be sure to hold the dotted quarter note in measure 4 for the full three beats. On beats 4 and 5 get set for the pick-up on beat 6 so your entrance will be soft yet audible. In measure 7 trill on beats 1 and 4 for the length of the eighth note only and stop on the principle (written) note before going on to the sixteenth note. You should be able to play about six notes in that time.

ILLUSTRATION 8

WRITTEN

PLAYED

Repeat the first section when you are performing this solo.

Measures 10-18 The second section should begin at a slightly louder dynamic level. Remember to make the last notes of each group of three slurred notes move into the next note. This section should also be repeated. "Ritard" on the last time through the movement.

musical term

assai   **very**

Measures 1-16 The last movement is again a faster movement and should be played with a full, rich tone. The quarter marked with a marcato symbol (>) should be accented but not short. In the second measure there is a new rhythm for you. It is a triplet which divides one beat into three equal parts. ♩ = ♪♪♪ Each triplet figure should be clearly articulated, but do not make the last note of the three short. Beginning in measure 5 there are two-measure motives that are exact repeats. The first motive should be loud and the repeat soft. Crescendo the "D" in measure 13 and play measures 14, 15, and 16 "forte". Don't forget to repeat this section.

Measures 17-44 The second section begins here with the marcato quarter notes as before. In measure 20 play the dotted eighth-sixteenth figure very precisely. There must be a difference between the triplet and the dotted eighth-sixteenth figures. Gradually decrescendo to the quarter notes in measure 29. These quarter notes and those in measure 31 should be played with softer articulation and held for their full value. Begin to crescendo in measure 33 to the "forte" beginning in measure 35. These quarter notes should be strong and accented. Play the two-measure motive in measures 39 and 40 softly and crescendo to the low "F" in measure 42. Make the connection between the low "F" to high "D" very smooth. "Ritard" on the last time through the section.

Sonata No. 5

Johann Ernst Galliard
(1680-1749)

M.M. ♩= 96
Alla Siciliano

(rit. 2nd time)

M.M. ♩ = 120
Allegro Assai

rit. 2nd time

Romanze

musical terms

allegretto	**light and cheerful; a little faster than moderato**
andante	**moderately slow tempo**

Although "Romanze" is a contemporary solo, written in 1975, it is composed in the style of the Romantic period (1825-1900). The primary characteristics of the music of that time were freedom of expression, subjective thematic material, and individuality of musical forms. Many songs of that period were titled "Romanze" and were generally pieces with a flowing melody, played very expressively and moderately fast.

This composition is structured as a theme and variations. The composer has written a theme, the moderato section in this solo, and later modifies or changes it. The chordal structure and melodic contour are kept constant while the melody is varied.

Measures 1-20 Prepare for your entrance while the accompanist plays the three-measure introduction. This time should be used to get the tempo in mind, set your embouchure and fingers, and take your breath. Watch the articulation markings carefully. Any notes that are not slurred should be tongued lightly with a legato tongue. Be careful to play all notes for their full value so this section will not sound hurried. Although the dynamic markings are specified, you should feel free to make variations of expression within small phrases. A general rule you can follow in this solo is that an ascending melodic line usually has a crescendo and a descending line has a diminuendo. In measures 5 and 6 the "D" and "C" should be played slightly louder. These notes are in a range of the bassoon which is weaker sounding. The performer must compensate by playing with more air pressure. The same thing occurs in measures 15 and 16. Practice the following exercise to prepare for these high notes.

PREPARATION 13

Measures 25-40 In the first variation, the "allegretto" section, you should play lightly and quickly to accentuate the contrast. The prominent articulation in this section is two notes slurred, two notes tongued, but watch very carefully for places where every note is tongued, or every two notes are slurred. Practice the following exercise using these three articulations.

The staccato notes should be separated and tongued lightly. It may help to imagine that these notes are bouncing. Remember that the word "simile" in measure 26 tells you that the articulation pattern using staccatos should continue until there is a change in the articulation.

You have already played the long-short-short rhythmic pattern that is used in measures 36 to 38. To start this section the eighth note is substituted by an eighth rest in the pattern. The following exercise will help you prepare for this rhythmic pattern in the solo.

PREPARATION 15

Play the "E" at the end of the five-note slur in measure 39 short, but not tongued.

Measures 41-48 Take this piano interlude as a time to relax your embouchure and fingers and to prepare for your entrance in measure 49. There is a slight ritard. in measure 48 in the accompaniment which should set the tempo for the "andante" section. Listen to the accompaniment rhythm to pick up the speed of the eighth note in measure 48.

Measures 49-56 Remember the one flat, "E♭", that has been added to the key signature. This section should be moderately slow but still moving. The quarter note that is tied to the sixteenth note must be held for its full value. Even though it is not slurred with the sixteenths, a light legato tongue should be used with no space between the figures. Play the eighth note pick-up slurred to the quarter note "forte" and the sixteenth notes "piano" each time the motive occurs. In measure 56 the notes marked with staccatos and a slur should be lightly tongued with a decrescendo and slight ritard. to end the phrase.

Measures 57-66 The original tempo of the "andante" should return in measure 57. Watch the dynamics carefully. In measure 61 the melody begins to differ slightly. Measure 62 should have a small "ritard" and a fermata on the first eighth note of beat 2. Take a breath after the fermata which will cause a slight pause in the phrase. The second eighth note of beat 2 is the pick-up for the end of the phrase.

Measures 67 - 87 The "allegretto" section returns in measure 67. Review the points already discussed about this section. Remember that "simile" means that the articulation should be played the same until a change is indicated. Begin to crescendo at measure 81 and build to "ff" at the end. Indicate the cut-off of the last note with a small up-down motion of your instrument.

Romanze

Menuetto

musical terms

ossia   **an alternate version, usually easier**
senza replica   **without repeats**

new notes

One of the most famous composers in music history is Ludwig von Beethoven. He was born in Bonn, Germany, in 1770. Although much of his musical training was sparse and erratic, he became one of the most brilliant composers and accomplished pianists of his time. About 1800 he realized that he was losing his hearing. He continued to compose even after his hearing loss was total and many of his last works were considered his best.

He is usually placed in the Classical period (c. 1750-1830), but his music represents the culmination of the Classical period and an important bridge to Romanticism. He used classical forms as his basis but expanded the harmonies and expressions much beyond his predecessors.

This solo is an arrangement of one movement of a piano sonata written around 1800. Beethoven's piano sonatas were evenly divided between three- and four-movement forms. The style and tempos of these movements varied showing his wish to correlate the movements to the expression he was projecting. In this sonata the third movement is a minuet-trio. This is a light, moderate piece in 3/4 or 3/8. Originally it was a French dance and was later developed into the minuet-trio form in sonatas and symphonies. The minuet was repeated after the trio developing the ternary, Minuet-Trio-Minuet, form.

Measures 1-8   The minuet begins with the pick-ups to measure 1 and lasts until measure 30. It should be played in a very flowing, legato manner. Follow the dynamics carefully to help you play the phrases more musically. In measure 1 and several other places, there are grace notes. Remember that these notes should be played just ahead of the beat and slurred to the next note, which comes on the beat. Count very carefully so that the dotted eighth-sixteenth note pattern is precise. Whenever this pattern is not slurred, put a slight space between the dotted eighth and sixteenth note.

In measure 4 the solo part moves into the tenor clef. Remember to keep the stepwise motion of the melody in your mind when playing in the tenor clef.

Measures 17-30 The original theme returns in this measure to finish the minuet section. When you are performing, all repeats should be played.

Measures 9-16 A second theme is introduced in this section. It should be slightly detached. In measure 10 be sure that the "C" on the last half of beat 3 is played as a short eighth note, not a sixteenth. The pick-ups for measure 15 are similar. Be sure that the eighth note is played for its full value. You should be able to hear the difference between this and the dotted eighth and sixteenth figure which follows.

Measures 31-40 The trio section, a contrasting melody, begins in measure 31. The running sixteenth notes must be played smoothly and evenly with a full, rich tone. Practice the following exercise slowly with the metronome. Strive to play as many measures as possible on one breath with a full, rich tone. This will increase your breath support. After you can play the exercise slowly, gradually increase the tempo to the speed of the solo.

PREPARATION 17

Above measure 37 you will see a passage marked "ossia". This is another version of the melody which is easier. You should use whichever ending you can play easily and smoothly.

be repeated when you are performing the solo. At the end of measure 48 you'll see "D. C. senza replica". This tells you to go back to the beginning and play to the word "Fine" without playing any repeats. This is the common practice for the minuet-trio form.

Measures 40-48 The accompaniment picks up the trio melody for a few measures. Take this time to relax your fingers and embouchure, draw any excess moisture from the reed quietly, and prepare for your entrance in measure 43. These two parts of the trio section should

Measures 1-30 Observe all suggestions discussed above. Remember to play the rhythmic figures precisely and to pay attention to all articulation and dynamic markings.

Menuetto
Piano Sonata no. 11, op. 22

Ludwig Van Beethoven
(1770-1827)

Two Impromptus

musical terms

con flessibilita   **with flexibility**
sub.   **subito, suddenly**
molto   **much**

Contemporary music embodies a number of different styles. All of the techniques that had been developed in the Romantic period were continually used, but new sounds and techniques were explored. The movement away from traditional harmonies was quite apparent. New scales were formed and established folk melodies were used as a harmonic basis. Rhythms were expanded to include different signatures and mixed meters.

These "Two Impromptus" are an example of contemporary music. Most evident is the composer's use of mixed meters and interesting rhythms in each section. These two are also composed of two different scales constructed of eight tones. These are called octatonic scales.

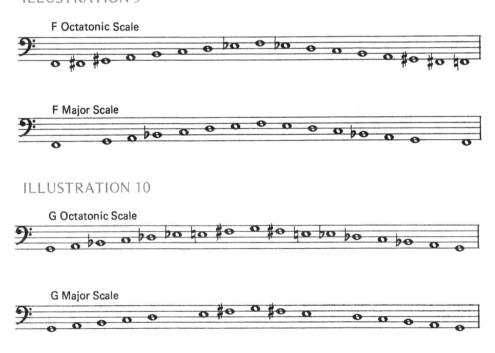

ILLUSTRATION 9

F Octatonic Scale

F Major Scale

ILLUSTRATION 10

G Octatonic Scale

G Major Scale

Measures 1-16 The first impromptu is a slow, lyrical piece. Play with a broad, flowing line and watch all dynamic markings carefully. The metronome marking is ♩=50. The changes of meter are based upon the value of the quarter note. Keep that rhythm in your mind and put 3, 4, 5, or 6 beats to a measure depending on the time signature.

Your accompanist begins the piece alone. To establish the tempo in your mind listen to the four quarter notes on the last four beats of measure 3. The indication of "con flessibilita" and "espressivo" tells you to play with expression and flexibility, not in a strict tempo. Study the movement of the melody for the small crescendos and decrescendos in the overall phrase.

In measure 15 the time signature changes to 5/8 which tells you there are five beats in a measure and an eighth note gets one beat. You'll notice the marking ♪ = ♪. The eighth note of measure 14 is equal to the eighth note of measure 15. Since measure 14 is continuous eighth notes, keep the rhythm in your mind and give the first note of measure 15 ("G♯") two eighth note beats and the second note ("C") three eighth note beats. Practice the following exercise using different meters and note values.

PREPARATION 18

In measure 16 the time signature is 5/4 and it may help to keep the eighth note as a reference. The dotted half note in measure 16 would be equal to six eighth notes. The accompaniment picks up the motion with quarter notes on the last two beats of the measure. These notes serve as a cue for your entrance in measure 17.

Measures 17 - 22 A new phrase begins in this measure. Watch the dynamics carefully for nuances (slight crescendos and diminuendos within a phrase). In measure 20 there is a new rhythm, a quarter note triplet. This figure divides a half note into three equal quarter notes. ♩=♩♩♩ It may be easier to think of this triplet as divided into two eighth note triplets. A quarter note would fall on the first, third, and fifth eighth notes. The illustration below shows measure 20 with eighth notes indicated below the measure.

ILLUSTRATION 11

Practice the following exercise using quarter note triplets. At first the triplet will be written as two eighth note triplets with ties.

PREPARATION 19

Measures 23-31 In this phrase the eighth note triplet divides a quarter note into three equal parts. The triplet in this measure comes on the fifth beat of the measure. Begin to crescendo to the "F" in measure 24. In measure 25 the marking "sub. *mp*" tells you to immediately play medium soft. Starting in measure 26 begin to crescendo to the high "G♯" in measure 28. This is the highest point in the first impromptu and should be played with a full, rich tone.

Measures 32-42 After the fermata in measure 31 the accompanist begins the last phrase. Again take your cue from the speed of the quarter notes in measure 32. Since this phrase is soft and sustained, take deep breaths so you will have enough air to support the tones. At the end you should give the cut-off for you and your accompanist.

musical term

scherzando   **playfully**

To contrast with the first impromptu, the second one is light, detached, and a little faster. The staccatos must be short and crisp. Think of these as if they were bouncing. Notice that the metronome marking is ♩. = 72. The basic beat for the second impromptu is the eighth note, so divide the dotted quarter note into three eighth note pulses. Look at the time signature changes and put either 5 or 6 beats in a measure. The accompanist will start the piece and set the tempo for you. To help prepare for the various rhythmic patterns used in this solo, practice the following exercise.

PREPARATION 20

In the exercise above and in the solo, watch the articulation marks, especially the figures that are slurred. Begin the solo softly and gradually start to crescendo in measure 11. Measure 12 should be "forte" with a slight accent on the tenuto "D♯".

Measures 14-22 Begin this phrase "forte", but keep the staccatos light. Gradually crescendo to the high "F♯" in measure 20 and decrescendo to measure 22.

Measures 23-31 In measure 23 there is a change of style. It should be soft, lyrical, and smooth. Crescendo into measure 30 and slightly accent the last note of the measure.

Measures 32-43 Beginning in this phrase the music moves to the tenor clef. For review of the tenor clef, practice the following exercise.

PREPARATION 21

In measure 40 the first note is in the tenor clef and the other two move back to the bass clef. Learn what the tenor clef note is so there is no hesitation between the notes. Decrescendo and slow down gradually in measures 42 and 43.

Measures 44-52 A part of the first theme is re-introduced in this measure. Be sure you and your accompanist return

to the tempo that preceded the "rit.". Keep the staccatos light and bouncy from here until the end.

Measures 53-59 Begin this last phrase "piano" and crescendo to the high "G" in measure 56. On the long "G" in the last four measures, keep the tone full and rich while you decrescendo from "ff" to "p" at the end. Do not slow down at the end. In order to release the last note precisely, be sure to listen to your accompanist.

Two Impromptus

Edmund J. Siennicki

fingering chart

(Notes in color are not taught in this book. Check individual solos for trill fingerings.)